...ld Bishopton, Erskine and La...

John Fyfe Anderson

The farmhouse of West Porton today is now within the boundaries of Bishopton and the land adjacent to this property today contains housing. West Porton Farm was one of a number of farms which was offered for sale in 1912, its area at that time being just over 206 acres. The farm buildings included a barn, granary, byre for seventeen cows, feeding byre for fourteen cattle, bull's house and stables with seven stalls. The farm also had the advantage of a free supply of 1430 gallons of water daily from Erskine Estate Water Supply. The sale document drew attention to the fact that it was surrounded by good roads in all directions and was near Bishopton where milk could be easily sold.

R34 was built by William Beardmore at their Inchinnan factory in 1919. On the second of July that year it became the first aircraft to cross the Atlantic from east to west.

Further Reading

J. Calder, *The Vanishing Willows*, The Princess
Louise Scottish Hospital. 1982.
B. Mackenzie, *History of Langbank*, 1981.
W.M. Metcalfe, *A History of the County of Renfrew*,
Paisley, 1905.
A.H. Millar, Castles and Mansions of
Renfrewshire and Buteshire, 1889.

D.M. Stewart, *Ye Anciente Kirke of Eriskyne*, 1915.
F.A. Walker, *The South Clyde Estuary*, Edinburgh, 1986.
New Statistical Account, *The Parish of Erskine*, 1842.
Third Statistical Account, *The Parish of Erskine*, 1959.
Erskine Public School Log Books: 1894; 1921;
1921; 1940.
The *Paisley and Renfrewshire Gazette*.

Introduction

The history of Bishopton can be traced to the time of the Roman occupation of the area in the first and second centuries A.D. A Roman fort at Whitemoss Farm was excavated from 1950 to 1954. This fort built in 85 A.D. covered an area of four and a half acres, holding five hundred men. In about 139 A.D the Antonine Wall was constructed. This 37-mile wall stretched from Bridgeness in the east of Scotland to Old Kilpatrick.

The Bishopric of Glasgow originally possessed land in the area. The name Bishopton signifies that the former Bishops of Glasgow had a farm and ancillary buildings along with the immediately surrounding area. The name Bishopton (or Bishoptoun) itself dates from 1332. The Brisbane family appear to have been the earliest proprietors of the original Bishopton House and estate, having settled in Scotland about the beginning of the fourteenth century. Alan de Brysbane obtained a charter of the lands of Muckerach in Stirlingshire from Donald, Earl of Lennox about 1334. The exact period when the Brisbanes settled in Renfrewshire is not known. Matthew Brisbane is the first member of the family about whom there is definite information. He was killed at the Battle of Flodden in 1513 when the Scots under James IV were massively defeated by the English forces which were commanded by the Earl of Surrey. Old Bishopton House was the main residence of the Brisbane family until the beginning of the eighteenth century when they moved to Ayrshire and the property came into the possession of John Walkinshaw. Successive owners of the house and estate were Hugh Dunlop, John, 12th Lord Semple, Hugh, 13th Lord Semple and Sir John Maxwell of Pollok who died in 1844. Charles Stuart, 12th Lord Blantyre acquired Old Bishopton House after Sir John's death.

Erskine means 'green rising ground' or 'green ascent'. The first recorded mention of Erskine is the confirmation of the church of Erskine by Florentius, Bishop of Glasgow in 1207 and Henry de Erskine was the first known proprietor of the Barony of Erskine in 1226. The Earls of Mar descended from him and the family possessed the estate until 1638 when John, 8th Earl of Mar sold it to Sir John Hamilton of Orbiston. William Hamilton, grandson of Sir John, sold the estate in 1703 to Walter Stewart, 6th Lord Blantyre. The Lords of Blantyre owned the Erskine estate until 1900 when William Arthur Baird inherited it from his grandfather, Charles Stuart, 12th Lord Blantyre.

The area in which Bishopton is now located was for many centuries a farming community where there was no sizeable village. The rural nature of the parish of Erskine underwent a great change in 1937 when many farms were compulsorily purchased by the Government in order that the Royal Ordnance Factory could be built. This factory, later owned by British Aerospace, was in operation until 2002. New developments have taken place in recent years. The computer firm of Hewlett Packhard Manufacturing Ltd. is now located on land which was formerly owned by Erskine Hospital. Ingliston Equestrian Centre has recently been established and is one of Britain's top centres of this type.

The history of Langbank is similar to that of Bishopton as its origins were a few landowners and large estates such as Finlaystone, Denniston and Newark which were established in the twelfth century. The area around Langbank was a farming community and its growth as a village only began in the 1850s. There were three crannogs or lake dwellings between Langbank and Erskine dating from the time of the Roman occupation. There was also a crannog at Langbank which was excavated at the beginning of the twentieth century. The Romans had a harbour at Langbank from where they were able to control the Firth of Clyde. John Knox, the Protestant Reformer, was entertained at Finlaystone House by Alexander Cunningham, 5th Earl of Glencairn, in 1556. A yew tree was planted on the west side of the mansion house to commemorate his visit. It was moved to its present position in 1900. Over two centuries later James Cunningham, 14th Earl of Glencairn, welcomed the poet Robert Burns to Finlaystone House. He left evidence of having dined there by scratching his name on a window pane. The 14th Earl introduced Burns to many people of influence when the poet was residing in Edinburgh in 1786-1787 prior to the publication of the Edinburgh Edition of his poems. Present-day Langbank is an attractive village, situated overlooking the River Clyde. Langbank simply means 'long bank', 'lang' being the Scots word for 'long'. The village has escaped the industrial development which took place in Bishopton and is a wholly residential community. Both Bishopton and Langbank retain distinct identities. Their residents have the advantages of a frequent rail service, nearby countryside and easy access by motorway to Glasgow, Paisley and Greenock.

The rapid development of the new town of Erskine has been a major change in the area in modern times. The keys of the first completed houses were handed over in 1971, but now the population of Erskine greatly exceeds the combined figure for Bishopton and Langbank.

Formakin House is situated a short distance beyond these ornate gate lodges. The mansion house was designed by Sir Robert Lorimer for John Augustus Holms who was a well-known art collector and also a stockbroker. Work on this property stopped abruptly in 1913 after Holms lost a fortune in a share deal. He never lived in Formakin House, but resided in nearby Gatehead House until his death in 1938. In October of that year an auction sale of his vast collection of antique furniture, silver, porcelain and tapestries was held at Formakin. In 1940 the property was purchased by Albert Ernest Pickard for £7,000. Later the house was converted into several apartments.

Georgetown Station was built near the Georgetown Filling Factory which commenced production of munitions for the armed forces in 1916. The building of the factory began in September 1915 when McAlpine and Sons employed over a thousand men on the project. The station platforms were designed to accommodate trains which carried 800 to 1,000 passengers and a covered passageway connected the station with the factory. The sidings could contain 120 railway wagons. This station was located on the former Caledonian Railway line between Paisley and Bishopton. Only a few traces of it remain today.

Dargavel House, Bishopton.

The original tower house of Dargavel was erected in 1584 by Patrick Maxwell. A slightly larger north wing was added to the property in 1849-1851 by John Hall-Maxwell. This was designed by David Bryce, who was Scotland's most famous Victorian architect and responsible for perfecting the Scottish Baronial style. Following fire damage in 1909, interior restoration work was undertaken by Peter Macgregor Chalmers. The last occasion on which the garden and grounds were open to the people of Bishopton and district was on 12th May 1937 when a garden fête was held to celebrate the Coronation of King George VI. Various sporting activities and games took place. Music was provided by Tollcross Works Pipe Band. On leaving the estate the children were presented with a Coronation mug as a souvenir of the occasion.

Dargavel House, Bishopton.

Dargavel House is situated about one mile south of Bishopton Station and this is a view of it from the rear. The house has been well screened by trees and hidden from public view for many decades. There has only been restricted access to the property as it was contained within the grounds of the Royal Ordnance Factory from 1937, itself acquired by British Aerospace in 1987. At one time the Dargavel Estate amounted to 803 acres. The last owner was Captain Alexander Hall-Maxwell, a descendant of the two ancient Renfrewshire families of the Halls of Fulbar and the Maxwells of Dargavel.

There were problems during the building of the Glasgow to Greenock Railway when the line reached Bishopton. The land on which the railway was being built, belonged to Charles Stuart, 12th Lord Blantyre, who refused permission for the line to be laid on lower ground near the River Clyde. As a result it was necessary to construct two tunnels through whinstone rock. The work on these tunnels lasted from 1839 to 1841 and gunpowder was used for blasting the rock. The rubble from the tunnels was used in building up the embankment of the line as it ran westwards beside the Clyde. A newspaper report of 1840 stated that there were nearly 3,000 men working on the railway. In addition, more than 200 horses were used.

This is a view of Bishopton Station in the late 1930s. On the left the sign reads : 'If you feel you need a change Bishopton is well within your range'. This advertisement was the idea of Mr. Matthew Woodrow who was the stationmaster at the time. The railway track leads from the station to a siding in the nearby former Royal Ordnance Factory. Trains operated from the siding until the late 1990s. The Royal Ordnance Factory had a very important role during the Second World War and for many years afterwards in producing munitions for the armed forces. The factory in Bishopton was one of the 44 Royal Ordnance Factories which were in operation in Britain by 1945.

The houses shown here, since demolished, were known as Rossland Cottages (this part of Bishopton once being known as Rossland) and situated in Greenock Road at the east end of Bishopton. The site is now occupied by Hamilton Bros. (Engineering) Ltd and it was where Peters' Garage was formerly located.

Apart from the large tree near the post office having been removed, this scene remains relatively unchanged. As early as the 1840s there were three deliveries of mail and three uplifts on a daily basis in Bishopton.

POINTHOUSE, BISHOPTON.

This semi-detached villa faces onto a traffic-free Greenock Road in this tranquil scene from the early 1900s. A stationary horse and cart is visible in Gledstane Road. Houses have been built on the vacant ground on the right of Gledstane Road and the wall on the right in Greenock Road has been removed.

The area in the foreground has subsequently been built over as housing development has taken place. The house with the gable end in the picture is in Kingston Road while the other substantial properties are in Old Greenock road, formerly known as School Road. This road formed part of the main public road from Glasgow to Greenock when it was used by horse-drawn traffic.

OUR LADY OF LOURDES   BISHOPTON

This is an early interior view of the chapel of Our Lady of Lourdes in Old Greenock Road. The building of this chapel was completed in 1926. In the *New Statistical Account* in 1842 the Rev. Robert Walter Stewart drew attention to the fact that there were only four Roman Catholics residing in the parish. The number of the Catholics in the area increased as a result of many Irish labourers remaining after the completion of the Glasgow to Greenock Railway in 1841. Originally the church and parish of Erskine was included in the see of Glasgow and would have been under the jurisdiction of the Bishop of Glasgow. From 1207 until the Scottish Reformation in 1560 the parish of Erskine belonged to Paisley Abbey.

A noticeable feature of this scene from 1951 is the total absence of traffic at what is now a very busy junction. On the left of this view is the former Erskine Hall which was financed by Charles Stuart, 12th Lord Blantyre and opened in 1889. He occasionally led religious services there. These premises were purchased by Erskine Parish Church in 1927. Recent major renovation has been undertaken by Bishopton Parish Church and it is now known as 'The Cornerstone'.

This view of the Golf Inn in Greenock Road dates from the early 1900s. The proprietor at this time was Mr. H. Munro whose name is prominently displayed above the entrance. In the 1930s the owner was Robert Waid. It is thought that the Golf Inn was so named because in the early years of Erskine Golf Club there was no club house and the players came to this inn for refreshments. The Golf Inn latterly was well-known for its real ales and only closed down recently.

This smithy was located in Greenock Road, Bishopton. The blacksmith's premises are now used as residential accommodation. In the mid-1930s there were three blacksmiths in Bishopton, these being J.C Stirrat in Greenock Road, A.Craig and Sons at Freeland Smithy and Daniel Hall at the Old Castle in Kingston Road. The services of the blacksmiths were in great demand when heavy horses, mainly Clydesdales, were used on local farms. By the late 1950s tractors were in common usage and the one remaining blacksmith did little shoeing. His work then mainly consisted of carrying out repairs and dealing in scrap metal.

ERSKINE CHURCH.

This church, now known as Bishopton Parish Church, was completed in 1815. In the same year the Rev. Andrew Stewart was appointed minister. He married the Honourable Margaret Stewart. the only daughter of Alexander Stewart 10th Lord Blantyre. Robert Walter Stewart, 11th Lord Blantyre was a member of the small committee which oversaw the building of the present church. The previous church on a nearby site was demolished in 1813 because it was in a ruinous condition. The Lords of Blantyre had a laird's pew in the gallery of the church. The funeral service of Charles, 12th and last Lord Blantyre was held here on 15th December 1900. On that occasion the Rev. William Ferguson referred to his lordship in the following terms: *While he might have aspired to some distinguished position in the service of his country . he contented himself during the greater part of his life with humble ambitions, fulfilling the duties of his station on his own estates and among his own tenantry and people.*

Erskine Parish Church is covered with ivy in this view from 1904. In 1915 the minister was the Rev. David Melville Stewart. At that time he delivered a series of lectures to mark the one hundredth anniversary of the building of the church. These lectures were published in a book entitled Ye Anciente Kirke of Eriskyne. The author dedicated the book to the parishioners of Erskine from whom he received *so much good will, among whom it is so pleasant to dwell.* David Melville Stewart was inducted as minister in 1913. He had previously been minister at South Queensferry, St. Margaret's, Arbroath, St. Matthew's, Edinburgh and Belhaven, Dunbar.

This is a section of Greenock Road at the west end of Bishopton, with an early car visible. The semi-detached property in the foreground has since been demolished and a similar property has been built further back from the road.

Two boys wearing short trousers sit on the wall in Greenock Road at the west end of Bishopton beside this row of well-built bungalows in 1951. On the far right of this view no houses have as yet been built in the field. The two properties which can be faintly discerned are in Old Greenock Road. In 1951 the population of Bishopton was 1,586. By 1988 this figure had risen to 5,610.

The bungalows on the left are in the Grove which is set back from Greenock Road. The properties on the right of this view are in Old Greenock Road. Three further semi-detached properties have been built in the Grove. In the foreground corn has been gathered into stooks. This area is still open space but no crops are grown on it now.

The hedges are somewhat overgrown in this view of a deserted Greenock Road in Bishopton. This part of the village is known as 'The Vales' because four houses in this location have 'vale' in their house names. These are Annavale, Lilyvale, Rosevale and Fernvale. There is a noticeable lack of street-lighting here with the exception of the imposing lamp at the entrance of the house in the foreground. As late as 1959 the issue of street-lighting in Bishopton was still a matter of concern as improvements were required.

This photograph shows a group of girls from Erskine Public School with their teacher in 1911. The headmaster of the school in that year was John Morton Duncan, M.A., who was appointed to the position in 1896 and retired in 1919. Mr. Duncan had previously been headmaster at Langbank School for eighteen years. He was the first headmaster to occupy the new school house which was completed in 1897. Many of the pupils who attended the school at that time lived on farms and had to walk considerable distances on a daily basis in all weathers.

A group of pupils and their teacher from Erskine Public School are seen in this photograph which was taken in 1925. The girl in the centre of the front row holds a slate on which the name of the school has been written. An extract from the school log book of January 1925 indicates that school attendance was very low as a result of an epidemic of whooping cough. Later in the year the school closed for the summer holidays on 9th July which was also the day of the prize-giving at which pupils were also presented with merit and attendance certificates by the Rev. Donald Fergus Ferguson, the minister of Erskine Parish Church. A feature of the school in 1925 was enrolment in what were known as continuation classes. A total of 23 students enrolled in these classes, the subjects being French, general subjects, music, book-keeping and dressmaking.

A group of children from Erskine Public School pose for the camera outside the now-demolished headmaster's house in Old Greenock Road in 1938. John Wilson Rowan was appointed headmaster of the school on 1st September of that year. A report from H.M. Inspector of Schools for the session 1937-1938 showed that the total roll of the school on their last official visit was 125 pupils. This report also stated that the premises and playground were far short of modern standards. Needlework and cookery were on the curriculum at that time. They were described in the report: *Instruction in needlework throughout the school is creditable. The time devoted to cookery has also been used to good purpose.*

Here we see a group of children from Erskine Public School in 1952. It is likely that the parents of many of these children would have served in the armed forces and in other wartime occupations during the Second World War. Now, many of the children in this group will be grandparents. In the early 1950s and for many years afterwards pupils from Erskine Public School proceeded to Greenock, Paisley or Renfrew for their secondary education. Some went to schools in Glasgow. Park Mains High School in Erskine did not open until 1974.

Erskine Golf Club was established in March 1904 but the club house was not in use until January 1905. This golf course was laid out by Willie Fernie of Troon, the cost being met by Mr W.A. Baird, grandson of Charles Stuart, 12th Lord Blantyre. The obelisk on the right was erected in memory of Robert Walter Stewart 11th Lord Blantyre who was a Lieutenant General in the British army and had commanded the 42nd Highlanders. He was also a former Lord Lieutenant of Renfrewshire. He was accidentally shot dead in Brussels in 1830. It was because he was so highly respected in the county that this obelisk was erected.

Erskine Golf Club has one of the finest courses in the west of Scotland situated in a scenic location by the banks of the River Clyde. Dumbarton Rock can also be seen in this view, from where in August 1548 Mary, Queen of Scots, as a very young girl, sailed to France in a royal galley which was sent by Henry II. The Scots Parliament in July of that year had agreed to the marriage of Mary to Henry's son and heir, the Dauphin Francis. The marriage ceremony took place in front of the Cathedral of Notre Dame in Paris on Sunday 24th April 1558. On her journey to France Mary was accompanied by her guardian, John, 5th Lord Erskine. The Erskines had a hereditary right to guard the person of the heir to the Scottish throne. John, 6th Lord Erskine was created the first Earl of Mar by Queen Mary in 1562 after Mary's return to Scotland in August 1561 following the death of her young husband.

Erskine House was originally the residence of Charles Stuart, 12th Lord Blantyre. His father, Robert Walter Stewart, 11th Lord Blantyre commenced the building of this great edifice in 1828, but it was not completed until 1845 and cost £50,000. After the death of the 12th Lord Blantyre in 1900, Erskine House was inherited by his grandson, William Arthur Baird. Lord Blantyre's only son and heir, Walter, the Master of Blantyre had died unmarried in 1895. In 1912 the property was purchased by Mr Thomson Aikman. As a result of the appalling casualties at the beginning of the First World Was there was a great need for a military hospital in Scotland for wounded servicemen. Mr Aikman offered the free use of the mansion house, garden and grounds for use as a hospital for the duration of the First World War and for a year after its end. However, it was purchased by Mr John (later Sir John) Reid for use as the new hospital.

Photo., Lizars, Glasgow.

The interior of Erskine House was furnished to a very high standard. Canadian oak was used for the walls, floors and ceilings of the main apartments. The quality of craftsmanship on the ceiling and the ornate lighting fitments can be seen in this view. The house contained over 75 rooms of which seven were large public rooms. In 1842, Erskine House was described as the most attractive building in the parish, the impressive nature of the property being particularly evident when seen from the River Clyde. Before Erskine House was used as a hospital for wounded and disabled ex-servicemen, there was a great auction sale there in October 1911, when much valuable antique furniture was offered for sale.

MAIN APPROACH, ERSKINE HOSPITAL.

The famous surgeon Sir William Macewen played a major part in the establishment of Erskine Hospital which was originally known as The Princess Louise Scottish Hospital for Limbless Sailors and Sailors. The first patients were admitted in October 1916. By the end of October 1919, 5,552 patients had been admitted with 5,250 having been fitted with artificial limbs. The first workshop was opened in the hospital grounds in 1917. Artificial limbs were made and adjusted in one of its three sections. Basket-making and boot-making were also undertaken.

Nurses and wounded ex-servicemen pose for the camera in this interior view. The excellent work which was undertaken at Erskine Hospital received due recognition. An official report by General Sir William Babtie in 1919 stated: *Erskine is one of the most striking medical establishments in Scotland, and is marvellously successful in its results; it has all the advantages that palatial accommodation, generous contributions of money, the highest surgical skill and appliances that mechanical ingenuity can provide*. Financial support for the hospital came from the people of Scotland and there were also donations from India, Brazil and the Philippines. In 1919 these donations amounted to almost £29,000 which was a substantial sum at that time.

Princess Louise Scottish Hospital for Limbless Sailors and Soldiers.
Erskine, Bishopton, Renfrewshire

The dark-coloured building shown here is the former Erskine House, later Erskine Hospital. The ancillary hospital buildings seen here have since been demolished and a new facility has been built nearby. Erskine House has now reverted to the purpose for which it was built, namely luxurious living, and functions as the exclusive Mar Hall Hotel. The hospital was originally named after Princess Louise who was the fourth daughter of Queen Victoria. The royal connection with Erskine Hospital has continued with visits having been made by the Queen, Prince Philip, Prince Charles, the Princess Royal and Princess Diana.

Erskine Ferry.

The Erskine Ferry waits on the north bank of the Clyde in this scene from the early 1900s. On the opposite bank the Ferry Inn is on the left and the ferrymasters lodge, today a private residence, is on the right. In past centuries at this crossing point there was a ford across to the north bank. Stone quays were built to enable carriages and carts to cross the river. As a result of the deepening of the river a ferry service replaced the ford.

In this scene from the early 1930s a group of men with their bicycles are boarding the Erskine Ferry on the south bank of the Clyde. It is very likely that they are on their way to work in the various shipyards which existed at that time on the north bank of the river. The Clyde shipyards were world - famous and by 1914 were building about half of the world's new ships. Then, the workforce, including those in ancillary trades, amounted to almost 100,000 men. Even by 1929 the number of new ships which were built on the Clyde amounted to one fifth of the world's tonnage.

The Erskine Ferry approaches the south bank of the Clyde in this view. Cars can be seen waiting on the slipway at Old Kilpatrick on the north bank of the river. During holiday periods there were large queues for the ferry on both sides of the river.

Many famous ships have sailed on this stretch of water. These include the *Queen Mary*, the *Queen Elizabeth*, the *QE2* and the *Royal Yacht Britannia*. all of which were built in nearby Clydebank. Many paddle steamers also sailed past here on their way to Gourock, Wemyss Bay and Rothesay.

ERSKINE FERRY RIVER CLYDE FROM SOUTH, OLD KILPATRICK   D 6467

The Erskine Ferry loaded with cars and also foot passengers is seen arriving at the slipway on the south bank of the Clyde having crossed over from Old Kilpatrick. In the background are the Kilpatrick Hills. This ferry was the last of a series of ferries which crossed the Clyde at this location and was in service from 1936 until 1971 when the Erskine Bridge was formally opened on 2nd July of that year by the Princess Royal. The need for a high level bridge had been recognised as early as 1934. However, the building of the bridge did not begin until 1967. It was completed without mishap. Tolls for vehicles were originally charged on the Erskine Bridge but these have recently been abolished.

This is the slipway at Erskine Ferry on the south bank of the Clyde where the chain mechanism can be seen. Charles Stuart, 12th Lord Blantyre, originally owned the ferry at this location known as Erskine East and also at Erskine West. In 1868 he raised an action that these ferries had been affected by the operation of the Clyde Trustees having lowered the level of low water in the river. The result was that the Clyde Trustees were required to lengthen the piers at this location 75 feet into the river. Lord Blantyre raised a further action against the Clyde Trustees in 1882 alleging that large portions of his lands had been badly affected by their actions. On this occasion he claimed £100,000 in damages but was awarded £12,000. He spent a total of 35 years in conflict with the Clyde Trustees involving him in considerable expense.

The Old Inn at Erskine Ferry was a favourite place for walkers. Many people from Glasgow travelled by tram to Renfrew and then walked to Erskine Ferry. From there they crossed the Clyde by ferry in order to travel back to Glasgow also by tram. The writer T.C.F. Brotchie described the road to Erskine Ferry in the 1920s in the following terms: *It is a broad highway with a keen surface, a rare tramping road. It is an old road, a road of memories of the old coaching days, romantic days, to the railway and airship generations.* He also drew attention to the fact that rest and refreshment awaited the wayfarer at the Old Inn. This hostelry was demolished in 1976.

In 1948 Old Bishopton House was acquired by the Sisters of the Good Shepherd and became a convent. A home and a school for girls was built in the 1960s. A chapel was also built and this was connected by a corridor to the main house. The home was originally named as St. Euphrasia's, but in 1985 it became the Good Shepherd Centre. In 1916-1920 there was an extensive programme of demolition and rebuilding at Old Bishopton House, parts of which date from the seventeenth century. A notable descendant of the Brisbane family associated with the house was General Sir Thomas MacDougall Brisbane (1773-1860) who was Governor of New South Wales from 1820-1825 and President of the Royal Society of Edinburgh from 1833-1860.

At the beginning of the twentieth century there were 69 houses in Langbank compared to only 21 in Bishopton. Only a small number of houses were built in Langbank over the next half-century. Seven were built between 1900 and 1920, twelve were built between 1920 and 1940 and only two between 1945 and 1952. It was the coming of the railway to Langbank in 1840-41 which was an important event in the development of the village. As a result a number of houses were built from the 1850s onwards. The residents were mainly businessmen who could now travel by train to their place of work in Greenock, Paisley or Glasgow.

The property on the left is 'Benview' in Main Road, Langbank. Attached to the house is Mr. Templeton's grocery shop. He was in business until after the Second World War when his married nephew began working in the shop. When Mr. Templeton, Senior, retired, his nephew and wife took over the house and shop which also served as the post office. They were in business here until 1960. The shop is now Langbank Village Store.

In this view a man and woman are seen standing outside Cove Cottage West, a semi-detached property in Main Road, which was the location of Langbank Post Office for a period before the First World War. This property is now simply known as Cove Cottage. The other part of the building on the left is Cove Cottage East. The land for these properties was purchased in 1849 by David More who was a joiner. The vendor was Duncan Darroch of Gourock and Drums.

The property in the foreground is 'The Croft' in Houston Road, built in the 1920s. The ground on the left was cultivated as a market garden from where produce was sent to Glasgow by train. There were also four large glasshouses and the original area included the land on which the properties of 'Alisheath' and 'Silverbirch' have been built. Behind the wall there is Gas Cottage or Gas Work House. There was a gas supply in Langbank from the 1870s and the gas works were in this location until 1932. From that time Gas Cottage became known as 'The Chimes'.

A steam engine of the Caledonian Railway Company on its way to Glasgow is seen here at Langbank Station in the early years of the twentieth century. The railway line between Glasgow and Greenock was opened on 31st March 1841. The building of the railway was undertaken in 1839-1841 by hundreds of English, Highland and Irish labourers. Joseph Locke was the engineer for the Glasgow, Paisley and Greenock Railway. In 1841 there were nine trains each way on weekdays. The local parish minister, The Rev. Robert Walter Stewart, strongly approved of the decision not to have trains operating on Sundays.

FINLAYSTONE LANGBANK.

The earliest reference to Finlaystone was in 1373 when King Robert II confirmed Sir John de Danyelstoun in possession of Finlaystone. It is thought that there was a castle on the present site in the fourteenth century. At a later period the Earls of Glencairn were the owners of Finlaystone from 1488 until 1796. George Jardine Kidston purchased Finlaystone House in 1882 and changed the layout of the grounds. In 1900 he commissioned Sir John James Burnett to re-design the mansion-house. George Kidston's granddaughter Marian married General Sir Gordon Macmillan. The property is still in the possession of the Macmillan family.

In this scene from the early 1900s riders gather for the hunt meet at Finlaystone House. The fox-hunts in the area were reported in great detail in the local press with certain prominent local individuals being named. A typical report is to be found in *The Paisley and Renfrewshire Gazette* of 20th October 1906 an extract of which is as follows: *On Saturday morning the air was keen and bracing and the meet at Finlaystone naturally attracted a fairly numerous company. Mr Kidston was in the happy position of being able to provide a grand show of cubs that had carefully been looked after by Stewart the keeper.* The hunt also met on some occasions at Bishopton Railway Station. John Augustus Holms of Formakin was a former Secretary of the Renfrewshire and Lanarkshire Hunt.

Ferry Inn, Langbank.

The West Ferry Inn was situated near Langbank on the main road between Glasgow and Greenock. The premises consisted of a bar, bar-parlour and two sitting rooms. In 1842 there was a ferry in the parish of Erskine which was known as the West Ferry. This ferry provided a connection with the castle and town of Dumbarton. However, the Glasgow and Greenock Railway Company were empowered to purchase the ferry from its owner, Charles Stuart, 12th Lord Blantyre. As a result of an act of Parliament the railway company were given permission to erect quays in order that a steam ferryboat could make the crossing over to Dumbarton.